YAR: ST

A VISIT TO GALÁPAGOS

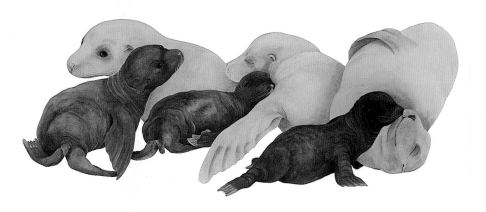

Katie Lee

HARRY N. ABRAMS, INC., PUBLISHERS

Previous page and back cover:

GALÁPAGOS SEA LION

Zalophus californianus wolle-baeki. Endemic subspecies.

Sea lion pups have a special scent that only their mother recognizes. Although they leave their offspring in the care of a "nanny" (another adult female) while they go fishing, mother sea lions are very protective of their young and will attack any strange creature that comes too close.

Editor: Robert Morton
Designer: Joan Lockhart

ISBN 0–8109–3928–2
Library of Congress Catalog Card Number: 94-70612
Copyright © 1994 Katie Lee

Published in 1994 by Harry N. Abrams, Incorporated, New York
A Times Mirror Company
All rights reserved. No part of the contents of this book may be reproduced without the written permission of the publisher

Printed and bound in Hong Kong

Acknowledgments

Thank you Carol Morley for teaching me that I could.

Thank you Carol Gracie for opening my eyes.

A very special thank you Greg Estes for patiently critiquing the paintings, for endlessly going over the text to keep it honest, but mostly for teaching me to love the Galápagos Islands almost as much as you do.

Thank you Jacqui Mudre for the wonderful photographs of my work in this book.

Thank you Susan Urstadt, my agent, for having faith in my work.

But most of all thank you Steven and Heidi:

this is for you as a small return for all you have given me.

Introduction.

Located on the equator, the Galápagos Islands lie about six hundred miles off the western coast of South America and are owned by Ecuador. There are thirteen major islands, six minor ones, and a great many named and unnamed islets. Recent discoveries indicate that many more islands once existed, some of them much closer to the mainland of South America. These have since sunk beneath the sea, but plants and animals on them presumably migrated to the remaining, "younger" islands and continued to evolve into the forms known today.

No one knows just how old the islands are, but it is now thought they were formed between five and nine million years ago, as a result of intense volcanic activity. They are still among the most active volcanic islands in the world: the islands Isabela and Fernandina have frequent bursts of volcanic activity. Many of the eruptions and lava flows add to the size of the islands by extending the existing land mass, often pushing the shoreline far into the ocean. But not all the land in this isolated archipelago was created by volcanic eruption; some was the result of oceanic uplifts, large folds of the sea floor rising above the surface of the ocean.

Though the archipelago lies on the equator its climate is much cooler than this latitude would suggest. The cold Humboldt Current passes by the islands as it flows north from Antarctica. As a result, the average air temperature in the Galápagos ranges from the 70s to low 80s Fahrenheit. The first four months of the year are wet and humid, and the remainder are dry and cool.

The islands were discovered in 1535, when a ship carrying the Bishop of Panama, Tomas de Berlanga, was blown off its intended course during a long voyage in the Pacific. The Bishop wrote of his observations on the islands and they thus became known. During the eighteenth and nineteenth centuries they became a haven for piratical seamen and whalers searching for sources of fresh water. These sailors also found the giant tortoise, which they realized would be an ideal source of food during their long journeys since the tortoises could survive in the holds of boats for a long time without food or water. The tortoises were hunted for many years, and their num-

An imagined recreation of a scene that surely took place many times, as passing sailing ships captured helpless Galápagos tortoises and took them aboard for food during long ocean voyages.

bers were reduced from probably several hundred thousand to only about 15,000. Three of the original fourteen subspecies have already become extinct. Fortunately, the remaining eleven are now protected.

Undoubtedly the most famous visitor to the islands was Charles Darwin. In 1835, during his five-year voyage on the English ship H.M.S. Beagle, Darwin became intrigued by the unusual diversity of species on the various islands. He observed that the isolation of each island had caused what were apparently closely related animals or birds to adapt their physical characteristics and eating habits in order to fill different ecological niches. (Among the discoveries of later biologists was that of eighty-nine species and subspecies of birds on the islands, seventy-seven are unique.) Darwin was only on the islands for a few weeks but he collected many specimens and gathered a tremendous amount of data that helped to form his theory on evolution.

In 1959, a hundred years after the publication of Darwin's landmark book *On the Origin of Species*, the government of Ecuador declared ninety-seven percent of the islands a National Park, and the Charles Darwin Foundation was created. In 1964 the Charles Darwin Research Station on the island of Santa Cruz was inaugurated. As a further conservation measure, the Galápagos Marine Resources Reserve was signed into law in 1986, sheltering some 27,000 square miles of ocean waters. Today, the Galápagos National Park Service and the Charles Darwin Research Station continue to work together to protect this fragile environment.

Shoreline and Lagoons.

The shorelines in the Galápagos archipelago vary considerably from island to island. Rocky shores of lava both old and new present rugged and irregular configurations, from hundred-foot high cliffs to low, ragged coasts. Also common are stretches of sandy beaches in an unusual diversity of colors, from seashell-formed white, to brown and black bands of pulverized lava rock, and even a brown sand beach tinged greenish by granules of a mineral called olivine.

Lava rock itself comes in a wide variety of forms along the shore. Some lava areas twist and fold like thick, black molasses that has been poured out on the sand and barely rises above the water. Others rise in sharp spikes capable of tearing bare feet; this is a'a' lava, named for a variety also found in Hawaii.

Along the shores of the islands are also lagoons, indentations of the coast that were formed when new lava or an oceanic uplift closed off an area of water. Fed only through narrow openings to the sea the water becomes brackish. There, in that still, semi-salty water, birds such as the Greater Flamingo find prime places for feeding.

SALLY LIGHTFOOT CRAB
Grapsus grapsus. Crustacea.
Playing tag with the waves is the favorite pastime of the Sally Lightfoot crabs. No one is quite sure where the busy little crabs got their names; whether it was from sailors who knew a dancer on the island of Jamaica with that name, or simply from the creature's quick, active movements.

11

LAVA HERON

Ardeola sundevalli. Endemic species.

Among the six heron species in the Galápagos only the lava heron is endemic to the islands. They love to eat crabs. Crouched down low, totally focused, the herons stalk along the black lava hunting down these tasty morsels.

GREAT BLUE HERON

Ardea herodias cognata.
Endemic subspecies.

Standing guard in the
shallow waters near the edge
of the beach, blending well
with the ocean is an
advantage. Quietly the
Great Blue Heron watches
as a wonderful variety of fish
swim right by its feet giving
the hunter time to select a
perfect morsel for dinner.

14

GREATER FLAMINGO

Phoenicopterus ruber

glyphorhynchus. Endemic

subspecies.

The Greater Flamingo gets
its wonderful pink color
because of what it eats.
Walking slowly through
shallow, brackish water with
its bill submerged, the bird
sifts through the organic ooze
at the bottom. Water and
plant matter filters out
through the fine hairs in the
bill, leaving behind the tiny
brine shrimp that form the
flamingo's favorite meal and
give the bird's feathers their
distinctive color.

GALÁPAGOS SEA LION

Zalophus californianus wolle-
baeki. Endemic subspecies.

After a hard swim, hunting
for small fish or squid or just
frolicking in the surf, it takes
a great deal of rest to restore
the oxygen supply and energy
for a young sea lion.
Youngsters may nurse for up
to three years and so remain
among their siblings and
cousins while their mothers,
who can bear young each
year, are looking after new
arrivals.

Sea Lion and Fur Seal. Fur seals and sea lions belong to the order of marine
mammals called pinnipeds. Because of the cold ocean currents surrounding the
islands, the Galápagos is the only place in the world where pinnipeds live on the
equator. Among the characteristics that pinnipeds share is that they have small
external ears and turn their hind flippers forward when moving on land.

Fur seals and sea lions look much alike, but are quite different. Fur seals are the
smaller of the two species: at maturity, they weigh between sixty and one hundred
forty pounds. Adult sea lions weigh between one hundred eighty and five hundred
pounds. Fur seals have thick, luxurious coats. Sea lions have a thin coat of hair.
Before they were protected, fur seals were a popular target of hunters. At the turn of
the century they were nearly extinct; now they number nearly forty thousand in the
Galápagos.

Both fur seals and sea lions hunt fish and squid, which are plentiful in the waters
around the Galápagos Islands. They do not compete for food, however, since fur seals

feed mainly at night and sea lions feed during the day.

Sea lions live in large groups on open beaches and around protected waters. They are very playful and social beings. Fur seals are quite shy and will dive into the water on the approach of another creature; they live in small groups on steep, rocky shores.

17

Katie © 1990

GALÁPAGOS SEA LION

Zalophus californianus wolle-baeki. Endemic subspecies.

Curiosity serves a sea lion pup well. In one year it will have to fend for itself. Raised in "nurseries" with other pups and looked after by adult females, sea lion pups usually only see one adult male at a time, the dominant male who serves as "beach master," guarding the females and young from attacks by sharks and jealously fighting off other bull males who otherwise live together on a separate bachelor beach.

GALÁPAGOS FUR SEAL

Arctocephalus galapagoensis. Endemic species.

Once they begin swimming, the main danger for young fur seals are sharks. Infant fur seals are not raised in "nurseries" like sea lions, but stay with their own mothers in small groups. They may be left alone, however, for as long as two days while their mothers go off to feed. On the mother's return, a bark-like call signals the youngster that its protector is on the way and it makes its way toward the sound.

Lizards of Sea and Land.

It is thought that the ancestors of the sea and land iguanas arrived in the Galápagos Islands on rafts of vegetation that floated down mainland rivers and out to sea. With few land mammals in the Galápagos, and therefore few predators, the newly arrived iguanas adapted to their new environment and thrived. Some remained terrestrial, while others evolved to become the only known ocean-going iguanas in the world.

Marine iguanas vary in color according to their native island. Some are dark gray to black; other are bright red and turquoise. Their powerful legs and large claws help the iguanas to maneuver over the lava rocks on which they live at the edge of the water. Marine iguanas dive as deep as forty feet when foraging on the seaweed clinging to the rocks. A flattened tail helps to propel them through the water and a blunt nose and serrated teeth are useful in pulling the algae off the rocks underwater or grazing on the slippery, algae-covered lava shore.

Marine iguanas range in size from one to five feet in length. Able to stay under

MARINE IGUANA
Amblyrhynchus cristatus cristatus.
Endemic genus and species.

At evening, as the sun begins to set, marine iguanas pile up together to keep warm. They are, of course, cold-blooded, but their body temperature drops especially low when they are feeding in the cold water. When swimming, marine iguanas do not use their feet, only a lateral motion of their tails and bodies propels them.

water for thirty minutes at a time, they reduce their heartbeats from something like fifty beats a minute to five. Without gills, they cannot breathe underwater, but draw oxygen from within their own bodies. The iguanas can drink the salty water, but they expel excess salt by ejecting a fine spray of saline solution from glands in their noses.

Land iguanas, brown and yellow in coloration, grow to be three to four feet long and weigh up to thirty pounds. Like their marine cousins, they are vegetarians and spend their days eating and sunning. Because of their size, they have few natural enemies, but domestic goats gone wild on some islands have dramatically reduced the vegetation they feed on. Land iguanas lay up to ten eggs in burrows during the dry season.

Smallest of the lizards are lava lizards, which eat insects. They lay their eggs in nests dug into the sand above the tide line. If a lava lizard is being chased by a predator it can break off the end of its tail, creating a diversion that may confuse the chaser long enough for the lizard to get away. Soon, a new but shorter tail is grown.

MARINE IGUANA

Amblyrhynchus cristatus cristatus.
Endemic genus and species.

The marine iguana's skin peels much of the time to permit the animal's body to grow. Scurrying in and out of the water on their own feeding rounds, Sally Lightfoot crabs scramble over the backs of iguanas and every so often will stop to pick off the dead skin.

23

24

LAND IGUANA

Conolophus subcristatus.
Endemic genus.

Pointed noses help land iguanas reach the flowers of their favorite food, the Opuntia (prickly pear) cactus. But to gain moisture as well as sustenance, they also consume the pads (leaves) and fruit of the cactus, sometimes spines and all. The spines pass harmlessly through their guts.

GALAPAGOS LAVA LIZARD

Tropidurus albemarlensis.
Endemic species.

Galápagos lava lizards have excellent eyesight, which serves them well as they hunt their meals of spiders, moths, and beetles. When defending their territories from intruders of the same sex, these tiny reptiles threaten by going into a series of movements resembling push-ups.

Land Birds.

Among the many things that surprised Charles Darwin when he landed in the Galápagos was that a particular group of birds that closely resembled the small common finch of the mainland seemed to exist here in a dazzling variety. Remarkably similar, the birds were largely distinguished by the sizes and shapes of their beaks and their feeding habits. Eventually, thirteen distinct species of finches were identified and Darwin's recording of this diversity and speculation on its significance contributed a great deal toward his formation of a theory of evolution.

Because these islands are such a long distance across water from the mainland, few tropic birds have independently reached them. Those that have found their way have adapted over the course of time to better make use of the limited food supply. Due to the largely arid nature of the islands, vegetation is sparse and restricted in variety. Insect species are not numerous, so land-dwelling birds have spread out over the habitats in order not to compete so directly with one another. Every area, from the moist highlands to the rocky shores, has its specifically adapted contingent of birds.

FLOREANA MOCKINGBIRD
Mimus trifasciatus. Endemic species.

Extremely aggressive, the mockingbird feeds on a variety of foods, from unattended eggs and the young of other birds to lava lizards. They live in family groups, which include parents, fledglings, and recently hatched chicks and together they defend a territory, which is unusual in the natural world. Unlike the North American mockingbird, they do not mimic the calls of other birds.

LARGE CACTUS FINCH

Geospiza conirostris. Endemic species.

A favorite place for the large cactus finch is among the prickly spines of the Opuntia cactus. Down inside the cactus blossom it finds the insects that provide its main diet. As its name suggests, there is also a small cactus finch.

MEDIUM GROUND FINCH

Geospiza fortis. Endemic species.

The big, powerful beak of the medium ground finch has evolved to crack open the nutlike seeds it finds on the ground. Two other forms (large and small) of this ground-feeding finch are known in the Galápagos, some native only to one or another island.

WOODPECKER FINCH

Geospiza pallida. Endemic species.

One of the few birds in the world ever observed using a tool to get food, the woodpecker finch picks up and grasps in its beak a twig, thorn, or the spine of a cactus to pry its insect prey out of their hiding spots, often under the bark of trees. Lacking a large, strong beak like a true woodpecker, the finch has adapted its behavior to become a more efficient feeder.

WARBLER FINCH

Geospiza olivacea. Endemic species.

The smallest of all the Galápagos finches is the warbler finch, so called because its beak is small and thin like a warbler's. This adaptation is used to pluck insects from leaves and lichens.

GALÁPAGOS VERMILION FLYCATCHER

Pyrocephalus nanus. Endemic species.

At rest and while catching its dinner of insects on the wing, the vermilion flycatcher glows brightly red against the lush green landscape.

MOCKINGBIRD NEST

A hodgepodge of treasures —twigs, Galápagos cotton, and a few leaves twined together—form a warm cozy nest.

GALÁPAGOS DOVE

Zenaida galapagoensis.
Endemic species.

With a turn of the head, the Galápagos dove seems like a glittering rainbow as sunlight bounces off its iridescent neck feathers. Like many Galápagos creatures, the doves seemed tame to early sailors because they did not fly away when a man approached, having no predators and having never learned fear. As a result, they were captured in large numbers for food. Their main predators now are cats, dogs, and rats, which have gone wild since being introduced on the islands by human settlers.

Tortoise and Turtle.

The Galápagos Islands take their name from the giant tortoise that lives there. Spanish sailors were among the first humans to arrive and the word for tortoises in Spanish is *galápagos*. Eleven subspecies of tortoises live on the islands, although there are only two basic varieties, those with a domed carapace, or shell, and those whose carapace is saddle-backed. The giant tortoises live on land; their cousins, the turtles, live in the sea and only the females ever come to shore.

An adult giant tortoise can weigh as much as six hundred pounds, and while no one knows for sure it is thought that they can live to be 100 years old.

Tortoises are herbivores. Those that live where vegetation is easy to reach have a domed carapace and a short neck. In areas where the vegetation is harder to reach the tortoise has a longer neck and the carapace curves up behind the neck so that high leaves can be reached.

Female tortoises nest during the rainy season. They dig a hole in the sand and lay between two and six eggs. The eggs are covered with soil and leaves and the female

GALÁPAGOS TORTOISE
SADDLE-BACKED
Geochelone elephantopus.
Endemic species.

The flair at the front of the carapace and the slightly longer neck of this tortoise permit it to reach way up to those tasty morsels high up in the vegetation.

departs. Four to six months later, the little hatchlings emerge. The first few years of their lives are difficult; no one looks after them and many don't survive. Once they had no predators, but humans and domestic animals gone wild became a great threat. After five years or so, however, the tortoise's carapace is strong enough so that few predators can hurt them. They are able to spend slow peaceful days looking for food or wallowing in the cooling mud to avoid pesky flies.

Turtles, like their cousins the tortoises, are reptiles. But unlike the tortoise, they are marine animals, seldom seen close to land. The female sea turtle only comes on shore to lay her eggs. A large hole is dug in the warm sand above the tide line, in it up to eighty eggs are laid. After covering the eggs with sand, the adult turtle returns to the sea. Months later, in the dark of night, the little turtle hatchlings dig their way out of their nests and make their way down to the sea. This is a vulnerable time for them, since they are virtually defenseless. Night is their only protection.

GALÁPAGOS TORTOISE

DOMED-SHELLED

Geochelone elephantopus.
Endemic species.

It is possible that this Galápagos tortoise is old enough to have seen Charles Darwin when he visited these islands in 1835.

GREEN TURTLE

Chelonia mydas agassizii.

Unable to stay under water indefinitely, the Green Turtle surfaces to take breaths, but it can swim or remain suspended below the surface for long periods of time. Females come to land only to lay their eggs, returning to the sea immediately.

© 1991 KK

Marine Birds.

Marine birds spend months at a time out at sea, much of it using wind currents to soar over the waves. They come to land only to mate, nest, and raise young. Because the cold waters around the Galápagos Islands support an abundant supply of fish, squid, and other pelagic life that can feed many species, sea birds come here at all times of year, not seasonally, and nesting activities among many species take place constantly.

Requiring little or no plant material for nest building, marine birds find the rugged lava shores of the Galápagos Islands, located as they are far away from land in the Pacific Ocean, an ideal nesting spot.

Marine birds were almost certainly the first form of life to arrive on the Galápagos Islands, and with them they very likely brought the seeds of plants from the mainland that may have become stuck to their feathers.

BROWN PELICAN

Pelecanus occidentalis urinator. Endemic subspecies.

Home is a pile of sticks in a salt bush, where hatchlings hungrily wait for their parents to return from a fishing trip with food. Both parents care for the young after they are hatched.

When all their flight feathers have grown, the fledglings will be taken out to sea by their parents for a most important lesson. By repeatedly diving into the water, the adults show the fledglings how to catch fish.

BROWN PELICAN

Pelecanus occidentalis urinator. Endemic subspecies.

Among the largest of the Galápagos birds, the brown pelican adult has a wing span of up to seven feet. Soaring up in the sky or swooping low over the water, effortlessly gliding on wind currents and exploiting its own momentum, the Brown Pelican surveys the sea for a fish. Spotting a school, it folds its wings abruptly and dives, splashing into the shallow waters and scooping up its prey fish in the big pouch attached to its lower jaw.

WAVED ALBATROSS

Diomedea eptorhyncha.
Nearly endemic, but also
breeds on Isla La Plata,
Ecuador.

It will take almost nine months before the chick in this egg will be independent. Among Waved Albatrosses, both parents share the duties of keeping the egg warm, protecting it, and later feeding the chick. Resting on the ground, not in a nest, the egg is moved by the parents as much as a hundred yards during the incubation period. No one knows why this is done.

When the hatchling emerges it is cared for in a "nursery" with other young, but each parent returns periodically, finds its offspring by call, and feeds it by regurgitating a fishy oil secretion.

47

SWALLOW-TAILED GULL

Larus furcatus.

The Swallow-tailed Gull is considered one of the five endemic sea birds on Galápagos, although they also breed on Malpelo Island off the coast of Colombia. Swallow-tailed Gulls nest on bare, steep cliffs overlooking the sea and often find themselves in the paths of lumbering seals making their way out of the water.

They are the only gulls in the world that feed after sunset. A reflective coating on the retina of their large eyes enables them to see even on the darkest night. Because they feed in the dark, the white patch on an adult's beak is important: a chick crying for food sees the white shining in the night, pecks at it, and thus encourages the parent to feed it, which it does by regurgitating partly digested fish.

FLIGHTLESS CORMORANT

Phalacrocorax harrisi.

Endemic species.

When cormorants first came to these islands many years ago, they had well-developed wings and were able to fly. But on the Galápagos there was no need to fly, no predators to escape from, and all the fish they could eat close by in the ocean.

As the cormorants became excellent swimmers and divers, their legs got stronger and bigger and their wings got smaller; the flight feathers diminished. Now the cormorants that live in the Galápagos Islands can no longer fly. When resting after being in the water, they often sit in the sun with their wings akimbo letting their feathers dry.

BLUE-FOOTED BOOBY

Sula nebouxii.

Developing its distinctive blue feet only when adult, the Blue-footed Booby male uses them in a mating dance to attract females. Strutting with tail held high, he lifts one foot at a time to show them off to their best advantage. He may also carry in his beak a feather or twig in his courtship, but unlike his cousin, the Red-footed Booby, he does not build a nest.

When the mating is successful, the resulting eggs are laid in a small depression on the ground and are incubated by both parents, who then later take turns feeding the hatchlings. The Blue-footed Booby congregates in large colonies (called booberies) during the mating and nesting season.

GALÁPAGOS PENGUIN

Spheniscus mendiculus.

Endemic species.

The only one of the world's fourteen species of penguins that lives north and south of the equator, this fourteen-inch, flightless bird makes a fine living in the cold waters that surround the islands. Swimming at high speed under water and using their feet as rudders, the penguins feed on small fish and return to land to dry their feathers. Like the albatross, the penguin mates for life.

LAVA GULL

Larus fuliginosus. Endemic species.

Only about four hundred pairs of Lava Gulls exist in the world; they are very rare birds, indeed.

The inside of this gull's beak is a beautiful red. Quite a contrast to the drab gray of the feathers, which match the color of the lava shores where the gull spends much of its time hunting for food. Scavengers, lava gulls feed mostly on dead fish and crabs, but are known to steal food from other birds.

BLUE-FOOTED BOOBY

Sula nebouxii.

These Blue-footed Booby chicks still depend on their parents to bring food from the ocean. When the chicks are young, the father takes on most of the feeding chores; smaller than the female, he makes frequent trips. Later, when the chicks can wait longer between feedings, the mother bird brings larger fish which they are then able to digest.

The chicks will not be able to fly until feathers have replaced all the fluffy down.

54

GREAT FRIGATEBIRD

Fregata minor ridgwayi.

Great Frigatebirds are kleptomaniacs; they snatch food from the bills of other birds as they fly home to feed their families. Not only do they steal food, but they also steal sticks from other birds' nests rather than collect new ones when making their own.

When the nest is ready the male frigatebird inflates his red pouch to attract a female who might be flying overhead. Male and female share in incubating the egg, and then one parent looks after the chick for a week or so until it can be left alone. The chick remains in the nest, however, for about five months and is dependent on its parents for a full year.

Plants and Insects.

With little moisture to break down the lava from which the Galápagos Islands are made up, the soil base is very thin on most of the islands. Cactus and Palo Santo trees predominate and all the plants have become modified to conditions on the islands. The Opuntia cactus has been so successful that it grows to the size of trees in some places. Only in the highlands, where a drizzly rain falls during the cool season, is there enough moisture to support ferns, mosses, and even a tree-sized sunflower.

In order to attract the widest variety of the islands' natural pollinators, most of the plants produce small white or yellow flowers. Though relatively inconspicuous, these flowers appeal to more insects and birds than larger, more brightly colored blossoms. The carpenter bee, for example, is responsible for pollinating a wide variety of the islands' flowers. The colors red, pink, and orange are not seen in the visible spectrum of bees, which are drawn to the color yellow. Birds and animals also assist in seed dispersal by eating fruit and seeds, which after passing through their systems, are

PASSION FLOWER
Passiflora foetida L. var. galapagensis Killip Passifloraceae Bedoca. Endemic species.

The flowers of this plant may look beautiful, but they smell terrible. This may be an adaptation to keep animals from eating the plant, thus permitting the fruit to mature. When the smelly flowers fade, the fruits become meals for birds and animals, who later deposit the seeds in new locations, spreading the plant far and wide.

deposited some distance away, thereby securing the plants' futures.

Because of the islands' distance from the mainland relatively few insects have arrived independently. Those who did arrive—borne on the wind, sailing across the water on floating debris, or clinging to the feathers of birds—have been able to adjust to life on the islands. The survivors not only are good pollinators, but have become an important part of the food chain.

SHORE PETUNIA

Cacabus miersii (Hook.f.)
Wettst. Solanaceae.

Hiding in nooks and crannies where moisture lurks and breaks down lava into soil, shore petunias are colorful additions to beaches and shores.

CARPENTER BEE—FEMALE

Xylocopa darwinii. Endemic species.

One of the few insect pollinators in these islands, the Carpenter Bee makes frequent visits to the Yellow Cordia plant. As it feeds on the flower's nectar, pollen from the anthers inside the blossom sticks to the bee's body. When the bee moves on to the next Cordia blossom, some pollen rubs off the bee onto the flower's stigma. This exchange of pollen fertilizes the seeds and thus enables the plant to propagate itself.

PAINTED LOCUST

Schistocerca melanocera.

Endemic species.

The most conspicuous and brightest of all the insects on the Galápagos Islands, the Painted Locust spends most of each day flying from bush to bush eating the lush green leaves of shrubs like the velvet plant. Male painted locusts make a "song" by rubbing their hind legs together, using it to announce a territory to other insects or to court females.

Following page:

GALÁPAGOS COTTON

Gossypium barbadense var.

darwinii (Watt)

At any given stage in their lives, Galápagos cotton shrubs show almost all phases of their growth at once: new buds, open blossoms, flowers past their prime, seed pods, and burst cotton balls can all be found on the shrub at the same time.

Katie ©1990